Adrift in a Sea of M&Ms
(Mixed race issues & Mental disorders)

Marcel "Fable" Price

Owned by disabled workers, NeuroQueer Books extends the
Autonomous Press mission: Revolutionizing academic access

Autonomous Press is an independent publisher focusing on works about disability, neurodivergence, and the various ways they can intersect with other aspects of identity and lived experience.

ISBN-10: 0-9972971-5-8
ISBN-13: 978-0-9972971-5-7

Cover art by Steve Weatherbie (Crossworm). Fable has much more to say about this artist, so go read more about him. Oh yeah, and visit his website. It's **www.Crossworm.net.**

Table of Contents

Without YOU this would not be possible...

This chapbook would not have been possible without the amazing friends, editors, colleagues, ruffians, artists and supporters that I am happy to call "The Squad".

This part is for them.
Feel free to reach out to them for freelance work, long walks on the beach, hot dates, or incredibly heavy praise – they deserve it!

Shawn Moore:
A phenomenal poet, performer, host, and person in general.
He carries a BA from GVSU and does a ton of freelance writing and editing.
He also works to spread community awareness for suicide prevention and crisis intervention.
Smoore.rambler@gmail.com

Kaira Williams:
A huge supporter of the Grand Rapids performing arts scene, avid blogger and a hilarious individual who has a level of writing only matched by her incredible high heel collection.
Read her snarky musings at **kairablogs.com**
You can reach out to her by email for editing or other word-smithing needs.
Kairawilliams84@gmail.com

KT Herr:
She crams a B.A. in English Language and Literature with a concentration in creative writing from Smith College into a body that contains the voice of a turtle dove, the writing skills of a scholar, and the outspokenness of a rebel feminist!
She is a great artist, editor and a pretty rad chick!
kt.herr@gmail.com

Tim Minor:
"You can just say I am a Double Major in Journalism and English.
Oh and I'm cool or something."

So there is that.
Oh, and he is a community youth worker, journalist, writer, editor, and a very captivating poet.
No big deal.
Majorminor87@gmail.com

Colin Smith:
He is an impeccable writer based in Kalamazoo. He is working for WMUK, the area's local NPR station. His super power is being an incredibly sick guitar player.
Colin.Smith11@kzoo.edu

Kelsey May:
Is a captivating writer/performer who is a member of our collective that does after school programs, assemblies, and workshops with the youth through "The Diatribe".
She is an incredible friend, a colleague, and a major inspiration to me as a writer. She honestly just makes me better, and I love learning from her.
She pushes everyone around her, and her organizational skills are unmatched.
She is a true asset to everything she is a part of.
She has a B.A. from GVSU in Writing.
Kelseyannemay@gmail.com

Steve Weatherbie (Crossworm):
Is a brilliant illustrator and also the magnificent mind behind the cover art of this chapbook.
Crossworm is an incredible artist, but an even better human, and a wholehearted friend.

This individual does far more than powerful illustrations, he is also the engineer behind the audio version of this book "#ProjectCastAway" (Which can be found on iTunes, Spotify, and also found on my website).

He has one of the most astounding ears.

His mixing and mastering skills truly brought this project to life!

Please look into this incredible humans work.

www.Crossworm.net

[Intro]

(Keep this in mind after reading each poem.)

Ever since we saw a poor Aladdin
caress cold brass
creating riches,
a Robin Williams-voiced genie
animated with a Smile
that will last longer
than the memory of HIM
Being seen as "Genuinely Happy."

Everyone has always wanted that
"One Wish."

I wish
I could get through this.

Trust me, you can!

I wish
Suicide didn't seem so appealing.

Remember, a robin flew to the heavens.
Please, make other plans. Keep Fighting
Through

I wish
It didn't happen to me.

Yet, here you stand.

Stronger, weathered,
whether you know it or not
others have experienced this process.

You are the driftwood
crafted from a hurricane of experiences.
no one the same,
bask in that for a while.

You are an example to others,
a masterpiece that proved
worthy of display.

Those skeletons hanging,
bring them out of the closet
accessorize them with new J's,
Some fresh shell toes, heels, or flats.

Hell,
put them in a picture frame.

Do not bother with a
"Do Not Touch" Sign.

Let the oils of people's fingerprints
Leave imprints
just as unique as you,
Leave the ripples on your open wounds.

I know crimson stains
same as fresh paint,
but don't be ashamed of the scars.

One day they will heal,
you just need to live to tell the story.

Promise me,
you will live to tell the story!

That you will encourage others
to do the same.

Your story needs to be heard,
believe this.

I know when drowning,
breathing is hard

or wanting to.

But promise me
you will be the Robin
once spiraling to the ground,
that chose to give flying another try.

Wishes are like prayers,
fueled by faith.

I believe in you.

[**Bubbles**]

This is for everyone
who hates

bubbles.

And I know you are thinking,
"Man, what is he thinking?"
But I am thinking
about how we were thinking,
as the pencil got to shrinking,

in those damn
bubbles.

I am talking about those
SAT
ACT
M.E.A.P. tests
that ended up leaving me
above the standard of stress.

Not over the questions
or the rest of the papers,
mainly
I just want to know
who vaguely suggested
the racial selection on these tests.

Let me tell you who –
someone who blew.

No really –
they must have had a
clean, clear, cut and dry view
of four and only four colors of d...

No, I'll stop.
But really, fuck that shit.
I am serious as a heart attack –
take a step back and really think.
As we all know, this isn't right.

Because unless you are
Black, Native American, Asian,
or White...
Then you might have had to select
the "other" bubble.
And who wants to be known

as an "other"?

What about the interracial individuals
torn between multiple bubbles?
Be that Asian/Black, Arabic/Black, White/Black,
or Hispanic/Black.
I mean honestly it seems to turn out like that.

But it is a fact that – if you are Arabic –
The Middle East is technically a part of Asia.
But people under the influence of self-induced
cultural euthanasia
might "accidentally" mistake you...
for white.

But who wants to admit
to some idiot in the education system
that you're Arabic,
So he can do something ignorant
like label you a terrorist?
So,
do you choose Asian or White?

What if you have never seen Asia in your life?
But you have
eyes like a Samurai, skin like the sun,
and hair like the night.

What if you're from Alaska?
Or the Philippines?
I mean, I would be confused
on which of those generalized four
bubbles to choose.

What about those from
Brazil, Puerto Rico, or South America who commonly
squeeze into a "Hispanic" bubble?
I have news for you,
these are not to be confused with Mexican, *mayne!*

Lastly,
what about the people
who have fully mastered the game
of race impersonating, maintaining continuity.
The ones from suburban and urban communities
with skin as pale as snow,
hair in dreads, fades, and fros
knowing EVERY rap song on the radio.

Because you are white
and whole-heartedly think
you are black?

Now *that* is an anomaly.

But this is not a "what if" poem.
It is a "hold up your fist in pride" poem,
"Because I know I am not alone" poem.

So, hold up the fist that you write with.
And swear to me now that next time you take a test,
you will fill in EVERY LAST BUBBLE
on that bitch!

Making them wish they had more.
Also hoping that you don't score
awful as piss.

But hey, then they will not know what bubble
to try and classify you with.

[Side Effects]

God bless America,
the only country that takes up
a *mere* 5% of the world's population.
Meanwhile,
unfortunately, also takes in 50% of the world's pharmaceuticals,
and 80% of the world's prescription narcotics.

Yet,
over the course of history trying to coin the phrase,
"We have turned the corner in the fight on drugs."

How?
Because we policed the urban areas,
until the prison turned industry?
While subliminally blinding us
to the fact that the real drugs
aren't being peddled from dark skin, or long rap sheets.

But from white coats, with script books.

Reading scripts slipped in from drug representatives,
reppin' drugs newer to the scene
than many strains police have ever seen.

Yet – don't you D.A.R.E.
Get caught with bud, bro.

With a quarter of some green, dank, purp,
loud, stank, chron, work.
Because depending on the criminalized city you reside in,
you might end up in jail.

Kind of funny how a substance
legal in many areas of the world,
is a crime in "The Land of the Free,"

when an Adderall can be prescribed to a 9-year-old
who cries and is told "sit still!"
Because the parents
measure their patience by the milligram,
and that is A-OK?

Unless you have it and *don't* have a script.
Then, it's a felony.
Pleeease!

What script do you *really* need?
The one written,
or the one typed?

Or the one that might sound,
and be read a little like an actual script.

"Do you have Restless Leg Syndrome?

You might if you are suffering from:
boredom, sore muscles, tired feet,
breathing oxygen, not wanting to breathe oxygen,
craving walks,
But not having the energy to go on the walk
you *so badly crave*
and could actually proceed to go on
if you would just get your lazy ass up, and go!"

"Do you have Bipolar Disorder?
You may if:
you want to smile more, you catch yourself frowning,
sometimes you are happy and others...sad.
If you breathe oxygen,
if you are human."

If you *are* human,
you know the power of the dollar.
And that green can even make HIV vanish
like Magic
Johnson's
hard on men glued to commercials perfected by marketing geniuses.
Making them want stiffer, longer, harder –
lives!

As they weigh out the pros and cons of side effects
they would never face
until they're sucked into a commercial that made it
so easy to relate to.

"But He... She... Looks so happy now!"

If you made 2 billion dollars a year...
You would have the ability to employ the best in the business
at pulling eyes, ears, and dollars out of wallets
even faster than Uncle Sam.
Because guess what?

They own him too!

Side effects you may suffer from:
bloody stools, hives, cancer, Lymphoma,

cold sores,
from or not from the person you felt you needed to make your life
'harder for.'

We are now so busy craving an easy fix,
tearing apart our well-oiled machines
for after-market upgrades,
that we are forgetting how much damage we are doing to ourselves.

Taking Alzheimer's medications with side effects of memory loss,
And anti-depressants that may spark suicidal intentions.

The outcome?

The leading causes of death in the U.S.
1. Heart disease
2. Cancer
3. Stroke
and
4. The adverse effects of medications.

We now live in a world that has become comfortable
with a mindset of,
"I can pay to fix what's wrong with me."

So,
besides being content
not taking the time to better yourself in a healthier way,
I would like to ask:
"What's wrong with you?"

If the answer is:
You don't know and you just want to seem as perfect

as the people in the ads you look up to,

Well maybe the things you should be adding up
are facts.

It hasn't always been like this.
It should have never gotten like this.

But where else can you get rich off of exploiting emotions,
and weak minds all held up by a crutch of convenience.

Only here!
So, God bless America.
But someone please help us...

We are sick.

[Little Timmy]

Little Timmy was only 5 foot 10,
a hundred and forty pounds of passion,
and known for laughin' –

like 10 minutes a day,
but that's a joke for every inch.
So don't get carried away
with the math.
The arithmetic is sick but so is he.

He hides scars so deep you can't see
the lifetime of emotion behind trees.

Two thousand, two hundred and fifty grams
crammed behind skin.
Sparked by his pen,
He's high as mountain
crests.
Ever-rest.
Never rest will he.

His dreams are so dark
that he sparks just to see
anything but reality.
And there is a Channel 4 fatality in his future,
if he fails to suture
all those wounds that left him in his room,
debating
if life was even worth it.

So

When loading a bullet into a gun of your past,
do you spin it?
Do you win it, if you end it before
your soul collapses?
This
revolver is a revolving door.
No drama but your mother, man, she can't afford
another casket.
The last pic
of her child in her mind, was a youth so divine his mind
was blown from new clothes.
Now his mind is blown from a snub nose...
Who woulda' known...

Who woulda' known that the world
woulda' missed his ass.
And that mentally he was more fragile than glass.
He was Bruce Willis fisted,
gifted with a right of Mohamed
but he could Ali over heads with words.

He
Tony Hawked linguistics.
That is, 900 degrees of touching people,
but it is a sickness that did *this*
crime
to a beautiful mind.
Mind blown open,
gun smoking,
walls painted red, but no joking...
The brain matter glittered like third grade pictures.

Or the young girls' faces who knew him before he faced this –
this time in his life,
where drama outweighed his mother saying,
"It's all going to be all right."

There are no more friends staying up all night,
as he chased them all away
along with his love life.
Pain,
strife,
That is what did him in.

It is a shame that in this world you either sink or swim.
And he knew more about sneakers than he did his kin.
Knew more about playing hard
than he did being a friend to anyone who ever loved him.
So in the end,
being hard is what will make you sink,
make you think,
Or make you blink at life.
Instead of keeping eyes peeled that day,
he blinked, and missed the love of his life walking away...

So

When loading a bullet into a gun of your past,
do you spin it?
Do you win it, if you end it before
your soul collapses?
This
revolver is a revolving door.
No drama but your mother, man, she can't afford
another casket.

The last pic
of her child in her mind, was a youth so divine his mind
was blown from new clothes.
Now his mind is blown from a snub nose...
Who woulda' known...

Who woulda' known
that the day of the funeral would come so soon.
It was the coldest day of winter,
held outside at noon.

No room,
just nature on his mother's knees,
and snot frozen on the noses of his brothers.
See,
every girl that ever loved him, they came to see
if the untamed man had met his own defeat.

But da-feet of his family were frozen,
while my eyes were glued *wide* open.
Watching people cry icicles and scream avalanche-causing echoes
this I will never let go.

But I do know
that it was all a dream.
And that guy inside the casket,
well, that was me.

I was 23 and playing Russian roulette with life -
the *gun*, is the thoughts that creep up at night.
The *bullets*, are the thoughts of
"Is it worth it?"
As my thoughts,

like me, seem so worthless until
the pen hits the pad
like the barrel of the gun hits the temple.
But damn,
until I meet my own demise,
I –
I'm just trying to open eyes.

[Tim Doe]

My friend Tim is 25 now and he's addicted to life.
But he's still living like
he's running from a prison -
might,
tuck away a couple cold ones after a hard night
of chasing pain
with way too much whiskey.

It's fishy how
someone so used to baring their soul...
could have NO control over nicotine.
Seeing dreams turn to night terrors.
Coughing till he wakes up.
Drinking till he passes out.
Yet –
he wakes up, ready just to do it again.
With all of his friends....
with,
with all of his "friends."

Meanwhile,
Tim saw his grandma kick the habit
before the bucket.
Trying to find good luck in it –
it seemed like a Fable.

Now, unable to cradle the memory of his granddad.

See,
it was too weak,
fragile.

He was too weak,
Fragile.
Saying,
"In two weeks, I'll dabble with the idea of a phone call."

But he dreaded hearing the sound of that machine,
breathing.
Filling lungs of a guy way stronger than he-
man.

Tim was more Wee Man,
a jackass in his prime.
Saying he's busy chasing dreams but still shortening his time.
Extorting his mind.

"But at least he's not snorting lines."
Maybe he lights the wick of that dynamite,
so he can control his demise.

Getting harped on to quit
by those who really love him.
Inside a tear falls,
but you can only see him smiling,
rolling his eyes.

Hoping they don't close –
hoping he doesn't fold,
with the same hand his grandfather played
but never owned.

All in.
Baby, he's all in.
Maybe he's all in-vested

in the stressors that're keeping it all in.
He's all in.
My,
my friend Tim.

My friend Tim is 25 now and he's addicted to life.
But he's still living like
he's running from a prison -
might,
tuck away a couple cold ones after a hard night
of chasing pain
with way too much whiskey.

It's fishy how
someone so used to baring their soul...
could have NO control over nicotine.
Seeing dreams turn to night terrors.
Coughing till he wakes up.
Drinking till he passes out.
Yet –
he wakes up, ready just to do it again.
With all of his friends....
with,
with all of his "friends."

With, all of his "friends."
He's just another shooting bar star,
dying in the flicker like his liver.

Wait –
maybe, he's not dead in this picture yet.
Or was it not born?

I can't remember...

But we heard
"A Band Called Death" blaring in the background.
They had a banner waving, dancing in the wind,
wow.

How symbolic, don't you think?
He didn't...

Netflix "A Band Called Death,"
"A, B, C, D,"
the (E)fficiency of them.

Them, symbolic.
Them, cigarettes.
Them, his peers - being sick of it.

It's all the same idea.
Different genre,
different years.

Ingredients:
Not listening to friends, or loved ones.
END
Ingredients:
Michigan talent cut short by a crutch that made it easier in the.
END.
Ingredients:
To not grow,
to not blow,
to NOT see your work as appreciated, even though some did.

He
was like the kid too slow to stop touching the stove
until he burns down the house he has always slept in.

He slept too hard
while he was slept on.
Leaving some saying:

"Maybe if he woulda quit, he woulda made it."
"He was jaded,"
busy thinking upon reflection's bastard cousin -
REGRET.
And I wish I wasn't regretting.

But reflection is more than something that shows appearance by the day.

Even if it wasn't – that metaphor would play,
a punk band would stay,
while a leader would still fall.
Both into history books,
the ground would break,
the casket draws
closer, as a soldier kisses his own flaws...
Like him,
like Tim.

My friend Tim is 25 now and he's addicted to life.
But he's still living like
he's running from a prison -
might,
tuck away a couple cold ones after a hard night
of chasing pain
with way too much whiskey.

It's fishy,
how someone can be so used to baring their soul...
Yet could have NO control over nicotine.

For a while now I've been seeing dreams turn to night terrors.
Coughing till I woke up.
Drinking till I've passed out.
Yet,
always waking up, ready just
to do it again.
With all of my friends....
with,
with, all of "our" friends.

Until the day
"A Band Called Death"
no longer plays my potential theme song.

I shall live a life style titled
Russian Roulette.

[F**k the Police]

Dear Public Servant,
who is a little more observant
of the man in the mirror
being a *little clearer*
than the broke-down-minivan
helping hand that WAS needed.
Wondering,
"Why is NWA seeded in the disc players of *thousands*!?"

As I was just tryin'a
Disc - Player.

Bouncing to Biggie Smalls,
flying down the Lyon St. hill to the disc golf course.
I then passed the 61st District Court
full of money snatchin'
lyin' snatches!

Can I get a -
"WHAT, THE POLICE?"

But now,
I am starting to realize that their location is kind of ironic.
because they are stationed on the corner of
Lyon and Ionia
and I am not *lying* just because I owe them.

But please,
if I can *at least* get an extension?

For me not mentioning the visual metaphor

I swear I saw officer?
No, I swear, I saw officer –
Mr. Blue Car, blue coat to match, black shoes,
do a bad move
passing up a clearly struggling couple on the left.

Smooth job, buddy.

I met, uh, four?
No, I met four people on the left.
Two were pushing,
one so cushioned in her car seat,
AND NO ONE LOOKING
to lend a hand...

Damn,
can I get a badge?
For turning my bike frame,
into a picture frame
that would hang in the hands
of a very confused looking 35 to 40 year-old,
African American woman.

As a guy with disc golf plans, clearly,
bag strapped to back,
bass now on Kendrick "Po-Up,"
NOW pushing a minivan,
hoping the police never show up.

As I got about three reasons warranting me
to be a runner in a Cops episode
or "Mug of the Week" in Busted Magazine's eyes.

Yet, receiving more love than I have ever seen
from this husband's eyes.

We had words in front of T.G.I. Fridays
And far from Lyon,
I was tired.

I said,
Hey man, how long are we going to push this thing?
The closest gas station is like 12 blocks away –
it's getting hard for me to stand,
why don't you just walk there
make it easier on your family
and get a gas can?

He looked at me like it was obvious.
Because, they don't just GIVE out gas cans, bro.

The 10 bucks I gave him was kind of selfish.

I wasn't gonna push that thing 12 more blocks
because by then cops WOULD have stopped.
Seeing
TWO black males,
one who disc golfs, and has plugs.
So, he must have drugs!
He's clearly a ruffian.

And although I was doing a good deed,
They would end up cuffing me in
with the man of darker skin,
who has a kid
and a broke-down van.

Many would assume NO money?
Police know it warrants MORE.

The Mommy is "out of sight"
so DEAD BEAT is stamped!?
Mommy is "out of sight"
so she is TRAMP-stamped?!

But she has no tats,
just standing blocks away with a church hat,
my bike,
and a very beautiful picture of me
as a person now in her mind.

[The Most Disrespectful Thing]

The 3 most disrespectful things
I've heard in my entire life
are as follows:

"You are the whitest black guy I've ever met!"

"Do you know what you need?
You just need a positive BLACK male role model..."

And last:

"I think he hates his black side,"
or in other words,
"I think he hates his own race..."

You don't know me.

And if you did know me
you'd know:

A.
If I ever see you in a cold dark alleyway alone,
I will beat you senseless.
"No shame"
type of senseless.
Almost as if to match the lack thereof
from the sentence you felt
needed to be passed on to me.

B.
I will beat you senseless.

C.
My *only* role model came in the form of a woman,
skin color irrelevant,
and if you've ever
put a hand on a woman –

Then YOU can come see me
refer to points A and B.
Because I was raised to believe you better respect them.

1.
Parental figure,
because the other left.
Leaving me with
1.
white step father,
who harbored his love for women
behind a red Chevy pickup
turned Men in Black deneuralizer – mind-erase pen.

I never could understand
why he drove with the heat blasting,
even in the summer time,
or why I could never remember
the car rides to the liquor store
to get dirty magazines and booze.

Losing track of miles
under closed eyelids.
As if the odometer rolling quicker
was triggered by the drool
that dribbled over my lips...

I still slip away in warm car rides.
Dreaming of one day implementing
A.
unto him
for never just focusing on
my
#1.

Hey,
maybe I do need that
positive *black* male role model.
Because the *white* one I had
sucked.

And the black one supposed to be there
pulled a Houdini vanishing act,
still to this day not seen.

But since then,
I've never met a magician that could impress me.
They always reappear,
making me think
"They just half-assed the trick!"

Now it's acceptable for me to be the butt of jokes.

I'm half black,
half white,
and 100% confused.
How tattoos
and what I choose to do with *my* body,
my clothes,

my speech,
shows less color because I added more.
But *off* a census selection!

Negating *my* ability in the eyes of many
to be more appealing to employers
due to my lighter hue.

I added a splash of blue,
and a dash of red.

So they shake their heads,
if I interview with short sleeves,
because I shortened my chances to get hired.

That,
that sounds like a color problem, doesn't it?

The real color problem
doesn't have a skin tone.
It has a mindset.
Thinking that it is the *only* one superior
and if that's you

I will gladly point you in the direction
of my shoes,
with the finger extended beside the index
and say
"Walk in them!"
"Talk in them!"
"Run in them!"
Like I have my entire life!

Avoiding *white* being thrown at me
in snowball fights of racial assumption.

Never hunting down my *culture,*
because it chose the door,
instead of adoring me.

I can't afford to hate a race,
or be ashamed of one.
Because it's simply a coin toss
but instead of a face,
I am facing a mirror on both sides.

It is not any race I'm hiding from
with the candy-coated camouflage,
and my stretched ears.

It is the marathon called equality
Where the quality of the people uttering,
"I don't care what color someone is"
becomes tarnished with a simple stranded driver...
Who looks *sketch* to you.
Employers,
whose definition of "clean cut" is a hue.
Lawyers,
judges,
Cops,
and my ex's parents' eyes,
vexed and scared with those sighs of,
"What're your career goals, anyway?"

It's getting old.

So is the next generation,
who didn't even turn their nose
at that Cheerios commercial
featuring two parents' colliding tones.
Exploding,
creating a beautiful little girl.

Who gets to smile,
with *both* parents.
Actually wanting to extend HER father's life.
Unjudged.
Just seen
eating breakfast with her family.

You know what?

I envy her.

[Afro Problems]

I'm sure you all have to deal
with some pretty annoying things.

But I bet you can't name one more annoying than:

"Can I touch your hair??
"Can I touch your hair?"
"Can I...
touch...
your hair?!"

"Oh my gosh,
THAT is so *neat*. Can I...
Feel it?"

Or
"I've been wanting to ask you all night... Can I..."

And *especially* the guy:
"Hey bro, this is going to seem really weird, but...
Uh, can I feel your hair?"

First off, if you include a
"This may be weird" in anything,
then it probably is.
But, while staring deeply into my eyes,
as if to hypnotize me –
then, it definitely is.

And secondly:
my nodding and smiling

isn't just to show off a grin.
Because really,
I would love to turn it around with a
"Can I feel your hoo-ha's?"
Or a
"Giggity goo!"

But truly, then
I'm the bad guy.
Because it's "just not the same."

Says who!?
I'm tired of getting my scalp caressed,
half the time getting less than a thank you.

And I'm hard pressed
to let some random dude feel me up.
I'm classy.
You can buy me a drink, and then
ASK me, sir.

But nobody ever thinks about
the oil sheen, treatment creams,
and countless screams I've had to endure
combing out knots on the daily.
Because YOU people messed it up!

And you're crazy if you think I'm going to let you mess it up
because YOU have a pretty smile.

I have hands too, God damn it!
And they like to feel, and touch just like yours.

And I might seem butt-hurt.
But really,
I just think it's a little bit odd
that instead of a nod and a compliment,
you were hell bent on getting your digits in this.

Well guess what?
Now so am I.
So don't act surprised
when I
Ask to grope you back.

[Don't Mind Me]

"This one
was meant to be quiet,"
said doctors about the child,
stillborn.
Moving.
Said factors about the lifestyle
I *still* live.
Yet –
soothing me more than the antidepressants.

Because isn't it depressing how life works sometimes?
But isn't it refreshing how life works some times?!

I'm sorry,
I guess that was the "bipolar"
When I can go from childhood memories of
Saturday morning cartoons –
understanding why I love
ninjas,
pizza,
and turtles.
To not understanding why life's hurdles
seem to match Berlin Walls,
as I've crumbled to pharmaceutical commercials.
Because the jingles over the symptoms
matched the dinner bell within.

And I've been *starving* to feel normal.
My own arm
always looks a bit more appetizing
when I feel trapped.
So, smother that?

No!
Where is the salt?

Because I know someone is willing to throw it,
and I might have open wounds that won't heal soon.

So,
if you are going to throw it
could you please pass
on the paper shakers?

It is normal to eat three meals a day,
and this would make a great one.
But, do we suffer from bulimia
if we're coughing up our differences
instead of our breakfast?

What's normal?
Because sometimes when I reminisce,
I get sad.

Is that depression?

Should life lessons be -

Forgetting that my step dad tried to fight me every day
Because a pill will fix that!

Erase the memory of my grandest father figure,
before he figures out
I just can't bear to see him
change with time.

I was told Alzheimer's would make him forget me,
anyway.

This one time,
or two times,
or three times,
I thought about killing myself.
A pill should fix that, right?

That's not *normal.*

But what is normal?

I hear the symptoms are:
Having both parents
happy and functional.
What you are seeing
is actually what you get.

Nothing grows graveyards in closets
the way locked doors and secrets do.

Because those skeletons,
if they admit their skeletons,
will be safely swept under the rug
out of sight, and out of the mind.

As if the blind are happier people.

Happy, that's normal!

And not bottling the-
"You won't, because you can't,"
or
"You are too_____ to do it,"
and the
"I wish they never, so I never felt,

not normal."

You shouldn't bottle,
unless it's prescribed.
It's - not normal.

Well, neither is having my disorder, apparently.
While for some scary reason,
I am labeled a 25th percentile child,
and the world isn't bipolar.

I ask then,
why does the globe have two?

I've been taught to think my emotion percent
is more relevant than my race
because face it,
with the globe being 20% black, 10% Hispanic, 12% Biracial,
I am forced to equally bandage my issues in the order of:
-Issue
-Get a tissue
-Race

Because face it,
I'm a minority anyway.
A 25% of a 12% leaving me feeling not even 3%

"*Normal.*"

But this,
this is for the paper shakers.
The ones whose hands match leaves in fall on stages,
Open mics, and to audiences
but don't –
because they aren't normal –

praise it!

Using crowds' ears like medication,
because it's cheaper!
Face it,
the only insurance we ever needed
was people showing us that someone
is willing to listen.

Genuinely listen.

And even if it's you, this one.
Keep your phone away.
But not the applause,
And look in awe at the people here
brave enough to feel
"normal,"
trying to feel
"normal."

My little brother is nicknamed after the prior
who was stillborn.
But HE –
he *is* moving through life.

A reminder to me
that being STILL
is *NOT* why we were born.

Life can SUCK!
But duck a punch and suck it up!
But don't sucker punch the ones lucky enough
to find their passion
in their sanity.

Their Doctor – a pen,
Their prescription – paper.

Chasing an eating disorder
by feeling sort of
"normal."

Have you ever contemplated suicide?
Do you ever get depressed?
Why at times does it feel like there is nothing left
when there is everything?

The same reason people pay no attention to art,
but paint.
Or pay to record but tune others out.

We all want good listeners
but can't do it ourselves so
find out the world's north and south poles are milestones!

And appreciate what you have,
no matter what it is.

Because sometimes you will be the only one who can, or will.

And there isn't a pill to fix that.
That is a fact.

[Did you know?]

Did you know
they made pharmaceuticals illegal today?

It turns out:
they are addictive,
if you take too many you can die,
they sway your mood,
they can impair your motor skills, driving, and even
alter your mind.

I wonder –
I wonder how they found this out?
How long could they have known about this?

Did you know?

Oh,
you did?

Well you couldn't have known
I was given early onset memory loss,
walking a straight line, heel-to-toe,
over desired memories,
proudly.
Laughing in the face of death, screaming
"WHAT IS THE WORST THING YOU CAN DO?
TAKE HIM?!"

But *they* took him.
They being the ones in my family
who act more denim than genetic.

And to this day
I regret leaving his side.

Mr. Doctor,
what part of my grandfather's being
helped you find and diagnose Alzheimer's?

I know an MRI can help you see the overall appearance of the brain,
But did you witness thumbtacks envying his sharpness?

Was it that he knew my mistakes before I made them?
And that he could play wide receiver
in family reunion football, and call the wide receiver position,
while remembering his high school routes?

I doubt it could be the steel vault brain
that contained generations of names
of people he loved.

I didn't shrug
when you started giving him the medication-
I cried.
Twice as hard when I was told
my name may slip his mind.

But I was happy finding his pain,
his fear in my life,
it was so clear.
I had to forget,
like he did.
Because he'd never,
so he chose to –
he had to,

so I did.

I find it deeply upsetting
that a side effect of antidepressants
Is feelings of suicide.

I find it even more depressing
that 1 out of every 10 of you seeing this
takes them.
And may proceed to have this on your mind.

Envision yourself on a roof, pointing,
with four fingers judging you back.
A vicious cycle of "I love you" notes,
as your digits turn to plucked petals in your palms.

You, not you, not you, not you, not you,
you, not you, not you, and 12 more "nots,"

But a million more "yous,"
Stressing,
thinking a pill can fix it all.

Just as Granddad never wanted to put a price tag on his mind,
but did.
Accepting the thought that a doctor
was qualified enough to evaluate him,
trade his memories for corporate-priced capsules.
As though his degree can supersede any doubt.

Not mine.

I find it deeply upsetting

a side effect of an Alzheimer's medication is
memory loss.

So if diagnosed wrong,
your family's name and birth dates might be gone,
but thank God for recovery.

Recovery,
Recovery.

We forget about that word.

But how could you ever remember
when they spoon-fed you the recipes to
forget.
Give you security to slip,
free fall into one's self-
doubt – not,
They will save you!

Because you PAID to!

Right?

Well I didn't
and I won't

but I will still smile!
Wishing I didn't make myself forget,
and push away so many faces
that I'm scared
I will not have enough time to pull close again.

But hey!
They made pharmaceuticals illegal today.
Who would have known they were bad?

I never would have guessed –
I forgot.
On purpose.

You may have as well.

[Aim at Houdini]

Aim.
Take a deep breath.
Let the air fill your lungs with life,
hold it for a moment.
Let only half of it out.
Focus,
then
slowly,
squeeze
the trigger.

Grandfather,
you might never hear this poem.

You may never feel this "Thank You"
caressing your eardrums-turned-well-weathered-spine,
clasping your ribs with a death grip like
a final hug goodbye.

"U"
"n"
"I"
Became ironic,

Those last remaining alphabet magnets
staring at me idoly for years,
Started to signify the bipolar smile of a boy
who was taught to love like a gunshot.

"Take aim."
"Focus."

When in a relationship with someone with bipolar disorder,
it is key to remember,
yet
so *easy* to forget,
that the letter "U" refrigerator magnet
can also be flipped
and mistaken with a lowercase "n."

But do not frown.
Better yet, with the assistance of periods,
Which can also be substituted
with the dots of two lowercase 'i's,
It can also be used to help erect a face –
looking at you,
displaying a mood
that you may not have intended to create.

To my dearest grandmother:
"U" - smiling -
taught me how to love.

Flip it.

"n" - frowning -
still - taught me how to love,
so flip it.

"U"
are also why I hate *them.*

"Them"
being overly constricting genes.
Not denim but genetic-
yet, still blue in the kisser
from holding secrets

like breath.

Wishing I could trickle crimson
from their zipper, locket always.

Mentally screaming STOP
every time I heard them
prematurely talk about my Granddad.

As if he had already punched his last time card-
replaced that overly used couch
broken in to perfection,
for a ready-to-be-broken-in casket
to – FINALLY – be rested in.

As I'm well-nestled in the memories –
still comfort, blanketing my mental,
seeing him magician a grandmother's frown
into blissful happiness
as if his fingertip
was a magic wand,
and her lips
simply as easy for him to alter
as an alphabet magnet...

Alone
"n"
always waiting for the
"U,"
Magic Man,
to turn it around.

As that is what would make
the memory of him everlasting.

Not focusing on the eyes,
"I"
could never see his gaze
sun-setting over the years

only picturing
'i's' creating smiles
from watching him rope-swing,
upper-casing smiles on our faces
through all of life's Ups and Downs.

You,
Grandfather.
Capitalized "I's"
not focused on the dots,
yet cultivating a pupil or two;
young Houdinis...
focused on creating smiles.

From
"n's,"

"U"
always turned it around
when I needed it most.

But now I

"Take a deep breath"
"Hold it for a moment"
"Let half of it out"

"I" find it so hard to keep wanting,
striving, working toward being

"U"

That at times, I just want to stop.

"n"

stay,
unprepared for this funeral
tidal wake of memories with my
"U"
being shattered into a past of window pain,
rear view mirroring my smiles

"n,"

my grandmother
being greatly concerned and inquiring if the reason
I push away women now
is because of her.
Because of my family.

Because I can only smile for so long
before I frown and utter

"Well yeah,
I can hear you all forgetting him."

Is that love?
Is that what you strive a lifetime for?

The "until death do us part's" true meaning?
Becoming skinny jean scene?
Seeing vows as a lifestyle
turning just another trend.

Making genes that much easier to split,
as a pair's seams.

I think they symbolize my loved ones.

"Hold it"
"Let half of it out"

Half of us now
see bipolar and depression genetically running in our family.

But,
so does pushing people away.

Through life, many of us have shoved pills into gaps-

into those empty pockets within ourselves.
But how many capsules does it take to truly fill regret?

And why use that when you could grab a shovel,
get your hands dirty and get
to the bottom of yourself
or others
by digging it apart?

I smile when I remember my grandfather
teaching me to love
over a Remington Pump Action 30/30 Rifle.

He Said:
"Aim."
"Let the air fill your lungs with life."

But all I can do is picture the leftover refrigerator magnets,
and fingertip magic wands

because his face in my mind
triggers too much of an explosion in myself to harness.
So I embrace the memory of his hands
and

"Hold it for a moment"
"Let only half of it out."

When I now slowly pull the trigger on life decisions,
especially
in regard to love,
I will remember how his loved ones treated him
like a quickly fading memory.

A bullet.
So easy to push away
and shoot,
letting the "Boom!"
resonate over eardrums,
that should have felt me saying "thank you"
a long time ago.

I could see him aim
me toward becoming a man
that could magician a frown into a smile.

And swear to teach my child to love
like a gunshot,
like the biological "Dad" I never had.

See, Granddad,

"U"
Taught me how to love
"n"

when doubt "n"
even still taught me how to love.

So Grandfather,
you might never hear this poem.

You may never feel this "thank you"
caressing your eardrums- turning-well-weathered-spine,
clasping ribs with a death grip
like a final hug goodbye.

But I promise before time fades,
or your grandson is settling into black,

I will thank you,
Magic Man,
for teaching me to take aim at my goals.
And how to perform life's hardest trick.
To love
The right way,
unconditionally.
Before it's – "boom" – Gone.

[Minute Maid]

The day I actually read the label
on a Minute Maid lemonade fountain drink machine,
my world collapsed.

The sky was arguably a shade of violet,
The grass a bit more blue.

Down was up, and up was down.
Life's ups and downs always seem to come around
when things just don't feel right,
ya know?

In not so fine print, it stated:
"0 % juice."
Zero percent.
Zero.

The epitome of "not even close to."
The big goose-egg, none, zilch, nada,
zip, nil, naught,
no way - is it in any way -
juice.

The lowest amount you could possibly have of juice.
That is, without it having negative juice.
Which in turn,
would actually have to contain said substance
then consumed by you for the container
to be negated.
Conveniently wrapped, stamped, and labeled
with exactly what they want you to think it is,
all the while calling it what it isn't.

Because I swear to God,
"Lemonade"
is made with lemon juice, isn't it?
It is Lemonade!

But today,
my world collapsed.
The sky was arguably a shade of violet.
The grass a bit more blue.

My world imploded from the truth-
out.
From a core burning with the urge to do better
for the world around me.
To live up to a standard I've printed on my label -
my work with the youth,
living, chasing passion,
and doing what I truly love
even if it's considered "taboo."

Her mother said,
"he's not shit -
he's trouble."
Striking the final nail with a,
"So how is that med student you went out with?"

She should have told her mother I was a doctor.
Better yet,
told her I was a dentist like her father.

Or...
Or maybe an astronaut even.
I mean, I am already well known for shooting for the stars.

So, I think I might just tell her mother when I next see her:

"I, Mrs. Myers am an astronaut!"

I have been one of those boys since age five,
manipulating toy jet planes,
into space-programing myself
to think I could be anything,
if I truly wanted.

If I wanted job security though, ma'am,
I wouldn't have set sights on the moon,
I hear they cut funding for NASA anyway.

But here on ground level,
They are still cutting checks to get the kids we work with
New computers.
New notepads,
And New notecards.

So take note
because I may seem a bit radical
but my dreams aren't of Kings, Malcolms, Garveys, or Ghandi.
But, if they were,
would having a diploma make them any more significant?

Oh?
Well, I am a dentist, too.

Not because I've mastered the art of pulling teeth
because I have only perfected the skills needed
for constantly displaying one smile.

I can masterfully pull your daughter's out at any given time,
even after the times when it was YOU who made her cry.

Maybe I
don't have a Doctorate,
but I am told I can shift a heartbeat with a microphone.

I can inject meaning into all of my interactions,
syringing heart-strings,
I doctor children's imaginations
into understanding they, too,
are just as instrumental to our future as any astronaut.
Using similar government funding to fuel their vessels –
still, unlike you, madam,
shooting for the stars.

Showing them
that a label has little to do with the contents,
and more to do with what you truly want that label to mean.

I want to know why we can't call garbage men pilots.
Those who
fly higher than their job description,
far above a title.
Probably
because they are *garbage men.*
And their job code is handling your trash -
your throw away, or careless toss around
which shouldn't include social judgment.

But it doesn't mean they aren't amazing.
Amazing fathers, teachers, lovers, brothers
or people who do a ton more
to directly better the world around them.

Way more than any human eye can see.
Because an eye can see a star

but it doesn't mean it still exists.

I've heard bodies make better doors than windows
But I'm no carpenter,
no contractor-turned-surgeon.
I have never had that stop me from looking inside a person,
seeing beyond the surface
and into the soul.

The day I actually read the label
on a Minute-made lemonade fountain drink machine,
my world collapsed.

It was the same day my Ex-girlfriend's mother said
I *"wasn't shit."*
That I am
"just trouble."

The sky was arguably a
shade of violet.
The grass was a bit more blue.

Down was up, and up was down.
Life's ups and downs always seem to come around
when things just don't feel right,
ya know?

But if you think for a second
that I would EVER trust "lemonade" that is zero percent juice
you are crazy!

It is supposed to be lemonade!

But guess what,
I STILL DRANK IT.

Maybe because it had less high fructose corn syrup
than the other drinks,
maybe because I felt like being a risk taker,
either way, after being labeled by you,
I no longer care about the ingredients,
and as long as it makes me happy
I will indulge.

This poem has everything to do with Juice.
But unless you know something about Ebonics,
Or 90s Movies,
this may seem to have nothing to do with *juice*.

But that's okay.
Label it,
label me whatever you like.

Knowing the once love of my life saw me as refreshing
is enough for me.

Drink that up.

Cheers!

[Native Tongue]

This poem

is for the kid in my 4th grade Social Studies class
who had the most awesome ponytail I've ever seen.

Who stood by in silence,
watching us with the most confused look
plastered on his face.

As the teacher spoke of
Columbus, freedom,
and the natives we "broke bread" with
to make this "beautiful" country we call home today.

We traced our digits,
with Crayola like lip liner,
letting our rash actions
speak louder than our words.

Refining our five-finger-feather,
construction paper headdresses to perfection,

erecting the idea through thought bubble, fall-colored high fives,
that Thanksgiving was built by acceptance,
understanding, and the idea of freedom.

Our teacher flaunting her incompetence
matching her Walmart-made Native Attire,
perfectly accessorizing her actions.

That day,

she taught us how to "rain dance."
We stomped around reams of paper stacked like logs.
Red and orange flames
crafted out of trees cut down,
dyed for our liking.

But
she actually knew what she was doing.
The technique passed down to call tantrums of passion
was spot on.

We kicked and we jumped, we danced,
hands flailing, to a cassette tape with light sounds of drums,
a soft hint of warm coals crackling,
and the rhythm of bare feet kissing the soil in unison.

Stopping only
to bellow the noises she taught us.

She said:
"A common Indian sound is easily made
from patting your lips and letting out a deep,
Ahhhhhhhhhh!"

So we followed her lead:
Ahhhhhhhhhh

moving our bodies continuously on a beautiful fall day,
hoping for Mother Nature's eyes to water
as she looked down upon us nostalgically.

Us, 9-year-olds, pure of heart,
minds mostly untarnished.

As if, in 4th grade,
we really knew what nostalgia even meant.

Each taking turns
running to the large windows
canvasing the south east side of the classroom,
soon to see the only pain undeniable
did not come from the sky.
The clouds were not gray,
with teary-eyed corners.

But the eyes of the boy of Native American descent
sure were.

Seeing the very rain we called for
rolling down from his "I have seen it all before" eyes.
As many others still let out that cry, that
Ahhhhhhhhhh.

Dancing,
jumping
and
unknowingly kicking him while he was down.

Our educator's lips lined with bittersweet nothings,
as a frown appeared on her ditzy
"Oops, I did it again" lips.
Accenting eyes lined with tears,
as the makeup of this child was
and will continue to be smeared socially,
for everyone to see.

We were taught that our makeshift headdresses

were traditionally made from not wasting
any part of nature's demise.

A give and receive.

Especially the beauty in between the earth and sky
that could be majestically cut
by a bald eagle's wing span –

but this time
substituted for mockingbird cutouts.
As we made a mockery of his family's traditions in public
school classrooms meant and regulated to be
"safe."

They should inspire, and nurture
instruct and not hurt or make anyone feel
uncomfortable in any way.

Little did we know
his family still practiced many of these traditions to date.
But in the proper way,
the real way,
the only way they should be.

He stood idle, watching us.
Tear in hand, crafted from our wasted paper,
from misused trees,
not even dying
But dyed for a consumer's liking.

You see, we aren't born ignorant.
We don't open our eyes for the first time out of the womb

knowing bigotry or how to practice injustice.

We are taught this
through public school history books
written by historians that the board approved.
Refusing to change the syllabus,
No matter who it wrongs
or teaches wrong
or makes us feel wrong about races and groups of people
who are born with the right to be understood.

We teach in an Un-United States,
through Un-American history.
Only including the minorities
when the month is tied to misery.

It is them, our fore-"fathers,"
that instilled the mindset that causes social blindness today.
But, it is us refusing to question,
although we've seen these hands raised since the 4th grade!

Acting as if we should keep our eyes straight,
because the palms are behind heads.

As his family's reservations
mimic our urban areas, under-policed,
as the drugs spread.

But these thoughts
are probably not in your head.
They've been going over it since youth,
in the form of a candid construction cutout
that was "fun" and seemed "cool."

It's not but,
do you know what is?

The coolest thing ever
was in 4th grade.
He was a boy of Native American descent,
and had the most awesome ponytail I've seen.
Skin
thicker than my plastic Ninja Turtles lunchbox
and had an actual headdress
he brought to school for show-and-tell day.
It even made some of us throw away our phony ones
made of belittlement and wasted nature.

I remember it because it was the same day
I saw the water we were taught to call for,
run down his "I have seen it before" eyes.

But, imagine if Columbus Day was really
"Show-and-Tell-the-Truth" Day.
Every day,
every month of every year.

I pray his children never have to see the same.
But KNOW
I haven't tried to call one drop of rain since I saw it fall from
his eyes that day.

And I am now teaching young minds to think in a similar way,
Imagine if everyone stepped back
and could form an unbiased opinion.
Imagine if no new mind was corrupted

from what our elders instill in them.
Imagine if our teachers taught outside the books,
Imagine if they could.
Imagine if they were allowed.

Only then could we show and tell the truth,
of what we could become.

Humane.

[Picasso Baby]

"We've become a country where
race is no longer so black or white."
–Lise Funderburg from *National Geographic*

By 2050,
75 million Americans will be able to identify with more than a single race.
Meaning most
will actually look a lot like me.

A Picasso –
once considered abstract thought, turned realistic present.

I am sure at one point; you have most likely heard people say:
"Those lips, with that hair?"
Or
"Those eyes, with that skin?"

"That is crazy, but it is not art!"

I personally heard it for the first time in elementary art class.

But
what if Pablo saw the future by gazing into the eyes of his paintings
showing him the mismatched features of
humanity and
equality in years to come?

A canvas strategically turned magic mirror, to hang on museum walls to
reassure
"Each and every one of you is the most gorgeous of all.
Ignore any rule, belief, or standard the closed-minded create.

Collaborate and you might make something

beautiful."

When my mother and my donor attempted their
recreation of "The Weeping Woman,"
the most common responses to the brush technique they used are:

"Where are you from?"
Or
"What are you?"

I now like to say that
Apparently, I am the future.

I am human,
before race was ever used as a chisel or a crutch.
Pre-whips, ripping open the midnight flesh,
showing starry, flickering eyes over
scars and hope that could be seen dying long ago.

Skin showed a journey.
It showed our ability to grow and adapt,
be it dampening the beating sun rays - *instead* of pride.

Or eyelids molded to an environment
with terrain too rough to take in with a wide gaze.

We have forgotten
that our days are numbered.
You can see the thing we focus on most is reflection,
instead of the direction we are moving.

Why do we so easily replace hope with hate?

Digging into our history books for life lessons of mistrust,
as if our great grandparents' parents' struggle
should trouble us today.
Yet, it always will.

It is apparent that some of us aren't ready to nurture the future.
We are so busy stringing up the past that children will never
learn to be monarch butterflies,
and break out of the darkness in a world that helps us grow.

Instead
we just train to be monarchs of government
because that is more relevant than evolving.

Dear caterpillars,
prepare to fly!

The U.S. Census predicts that by 2080, Caucasians –
those of white European descent –
will no longer be the racial majority in the United States.

And although you will never be able to debate facts –
one being that the majority
rules –
you can choose your voice.

I was once told,
"You will always be seen as a black male."

But I want to be seen as that butterfly.

Two tones collaborating past judgment
flying above a stigma.

Because, black is beautiful but
so are the other tones.
I want the orange in my wingspan to be *seen*,
not as an undertone,
not as an overtone,
but a stern tone of voice saying

I am, in flesh and blood, foreshadowing our future.

Instead of covering up my
"What are you?"
I want to be a *WE*.
A W.E.B.,
webbed - from Dubois to Marley.
from Barack to Malcolm.
Letting my Xs only be seen as a part of what made me.
Made me a lover of Booker T. Wash, Jimmy Hendricks, and Tiger.

Letting what mends the past
be the present of life that can tip the census.
The best
tip that changed my senses?

"You will always be seen as a black male;
you can only pretend to be colorblind."

And it is true,
because dark and light hues will always be more prominent
with *color* being a standard.

There will never be a bandage for racism.
But sporting the crutches after you've started to heal
is almost as bad as chiseling away the progress.
Walk,
run,
stay full stride in the right direction

But be weary;
we are still healing.

Because
Obama's skin is still seen as "the first of its kind."
Instead of
"the first of many to come."
So eggshells planted under the White House carpets
crack every time our nation blames "the one,"
the first,
the original spotlight, museum-framed, and featured Picasso,
who admitted to being a "mutt,"
as if NOT being a "purebred" is an imperfection.

Dear fellow monarch of another kind,

In 2050, I will be 61 years old.
A well-learned butterfly.
Waiting to be seen as one of many,
proud of my years of flying as an individual.

What is sad is that I will be able to say
"You have it easier now."
But what is beautiful is that I will be able to say,
"You have it easier now."
Nobody thinks you are too dark,

or too light,
or not right.

What's sadder is, if I say it,
I will be bearing the same chisel that will exist forever.

Weather the storm,
be great young caterpillars,
and prepare yourself to fly

free.

Marcel "Fable" Price
A.K.A. Fable The Poet

...Is a Bi-racial North American writer, teacher, community activist, performer, and motivational speaker from The Mitten State.

Fable The Poet is a Nationally Touring Artist highly noted for his work with the youth; spreading Mental Health Awareness using his own stories to consume the audience, and spread a much needed message: "At times, we all feel fragile. We are all paper boats entertaining the waves of life."

He is an official partner of Mental Health America, and has sat on panels across the country discussing the importance of discussing Mental Health awareness with our youth.

He is known across the nation for crowd-interactive features that leave those attending enlightened and empowered.

Acoustic, through written word, with musical backing, or even with a live band you will be taken on an emotional rollercoaster unlike any other you have ever experienced.

Buckle up, prepare to make a new friend, and enjoy the ride.

Contact/Booking:
FableThePoetBooking@gmail.com
www.MindOfFable.com
Follow the journey:
www.Facebook.com/FableThePoet
www.Twitter.com/FableIsTruth
www.Instagram.com/FableIsTruth